Student's Book

58 St Aldates
Oxford
OX1 1ST
United Kingdom

Beep Student's Book / Activity Book Level 2

First Edition: 2014
Eighteenth Reprint: 2024
ISBN: 978-607-06-0919-0

© Text: Brendan Dunne, Robin Newton
© Richmond Publishing, S.A. de C.V. 2014
Av. Río Mixcoac No. 274, Col. Acacias,
Benito Juárez, C.P. 03240, Ciudad de México

Publisher: Justine Piekarowicz
Editorial Team: Griselda Cacho, Rodrigo Caudillo, Diane Hermanson
Art and Design Coordinator: Marisela Pérez
Pre-Press Coordinator: Daniel Santillán

Illustrations: Gloria Celma, *Beehive Illustration*: Jim Peacock, Moreno Chiacchiera

Photographs: D. Sánchez; I. Rovira; J. Jaime; L. M. Iglesias; S. Enríquez; COMSTOCK; GETTY IMAGES SALES SPAIN/Robert Decelis Ltd; HIGHRES PRESS STOCK/AbleStock.com; I. Preysler; ISTOCKPHOTO; PHOTODISC; MATTON-BILD; SERIDEC PHOTOIMAGENES CD; ARCHIVO SANTILLANA

Cover Design: Leandro Pauloni

All rights reserved. No part of this work may be reproduced, stored in a retrieval system or transmitted in any form or by any means without prior written permission from the Publisher.

Richmond publications may contain links to third party websites or apps. We have no control over the content of these websites or apps, which may change frequently, and we are not responsible for the content or the way it may be used with our materials. Teachers and students are advised to exercise discretion when accessing the links.

The Publisher has made every effort to trace the owner of copyright material; however, the Publisher will correct any involuntary omission at the earliest opportunity.

First published by Richmond Publishing / Santillana Educación S.L.

Printed in Brazil by Forma Certa

Lote: 800381

Contents

0 Welcome back!......2
1 Time for School......5
2 My Clothes......13
3 The Weather......21
4 Animals......29
5 Jobs......37
6 My Free Time......45
7 The School Garden......53
8 The School Show......61
Festivals......69

Welcome back!

LESSON 1

1 Listen and point. 0.1

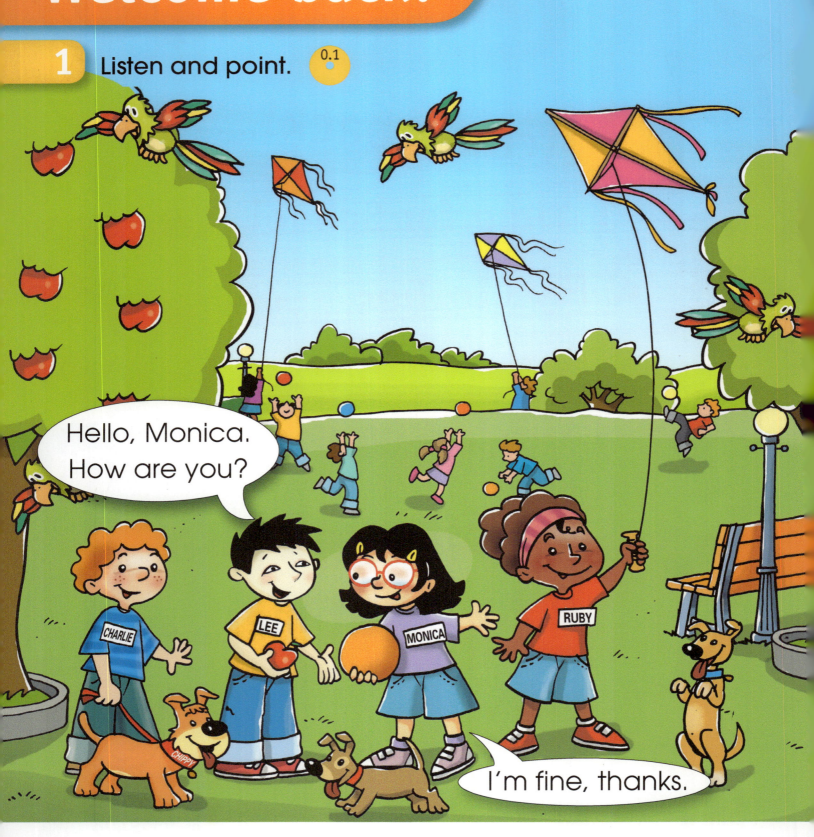

2 Listen and chant. 0.2

LESSON 2

3 Listen and circle.

What's your name?	Ruby / Monica
How old are you?	6 7 8
What's your favorite animal?	
What's your favorite color?	
What's your favorite food?	

4 Listen and sing.

LESSON 3

5 Listen and color.

6 Play a game.

1. Time for School

LESSON 1

1 Listen, point and repeat.

2 Listen and chant.

LESSON 2

3 Listen, point and say.

4 Listen and chant.

Where's the hamster?
Open your eyes.
It's under the plant.
What a surprise!

LESSON 3

5 Look and stick.

The ball is in the cupboard.

The plant is on the bookcase.

The schoolbag is under the window.

The teddy bear is behind the door.

6 Look and ask.

Hide and Seek!

LESSON

7 Listen to the story.

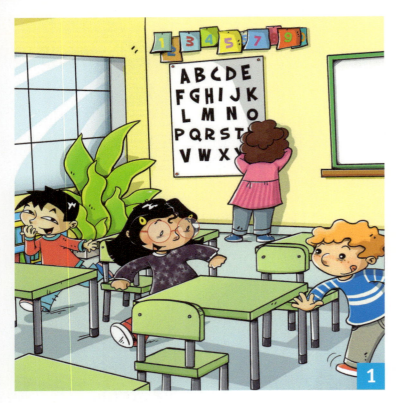
1

2

3

4

5

6

7

8

LESSON 5

8 Listen and sing.

Touch your nose! Touch your knee!

Clap your hands and count to ten!

Touch your ears! Touch your shoe!

Clap your hands and nod your head!

9 Listen and color.

CLIL

LESSON 6

10 Listen and match. 1.6

11 Make a name card.

PHONICS

Beep's World!

LESSON 7

12 Listen. 1.7

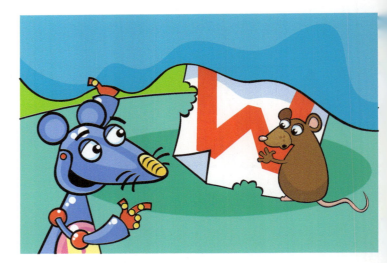
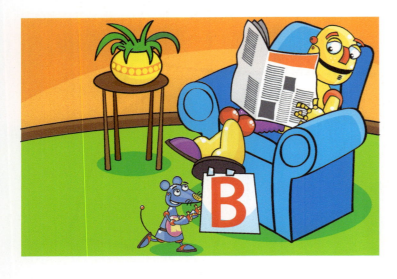

2. My Clothes

LESSON 1

1 Listen, point and repeat.

2 Listen and find. 2.1

LESSON 2

3 Listen and color.

"Lee, what are you wearing?"

4 Listen and chant.

What are you wearing today?
What are you wearing today?
Sweater and jeans, sweater and jeans.
That's what I'm wearing today.

LESSON 3

5 Read and stick.

I'm wearing an orange hat and a white T-shirt.

I'm wearing a green coat and blue jeans.

I'm wearing a yellow dress.

6 Ask a friend.

What are you wearing?

15

Monica's Party!

LESSON

7 Listen to the story.

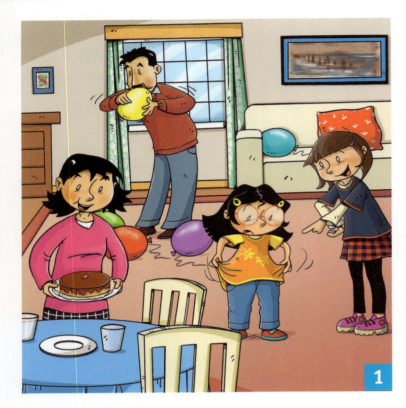

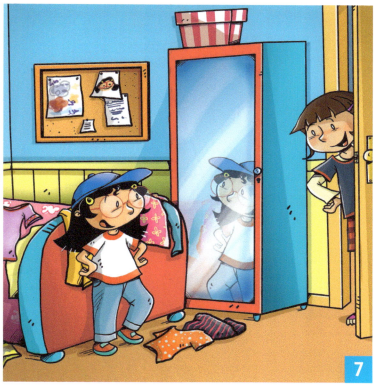

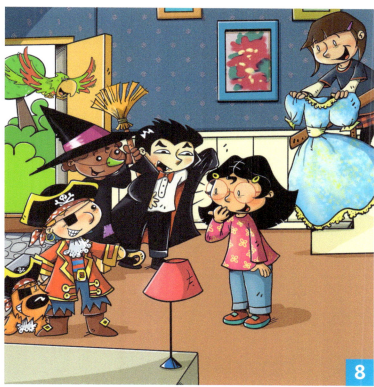

LESSON 5

8 Listen and sing.

Are you wearing green shoes?
Green shoes? Green shoes?
Are you wearing green shoes?
Yes or no?

9 Play a game.

LESSON 6

10 Stick and match.

I'm wearing a black hat.

I'm wearing a purple hat.

11 Listen and color.

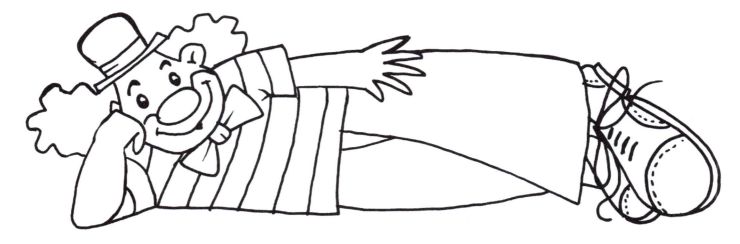

Beep's World!

PHONICS

LESSON 7

12 Listen. 2.6

20

3. The Weather

LESSON 1

1 Listen, point and repeat.

2 Listen and chant.

LESSON 2

3 Listen and number. 3.2

4 Look and say.

LESSON 3

5 Listen and sing. 3.3

What's the weather like?
What's the weather like?
What's the weather like today?
Go and look out of the window!
What's the weather like today?

6 Read and draw.

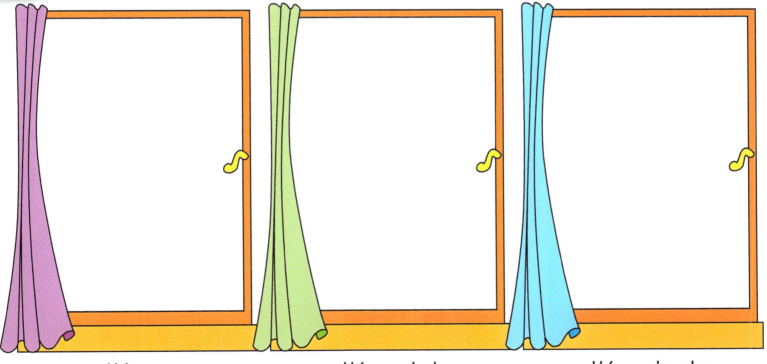

It's sunny.   It's raining.   It's windy.

The Snowman!

LESSON 4

7 Listen to the story.

5

6

7

8

25

LESSON 5

8 Listen and color.

9 Listen and chant.

Is it cold today?
Is it cold today?
Look out of the window and see.
Yes, it's cold today.

Yes, it's cold today.
So put your hat on,
And put your coat on,
And come outside,
And play with me.

CLIL

LESSON 6

10 Look and stick.

I'm on vacation. It's cold and snowing.
Daniel

I'm on vacation. It's windy.
Paula

11 Draw and write.

I'm on vacation. It's _____.

Beep's World!

PHONICS

LESSON 7

12 Listen. 3.7

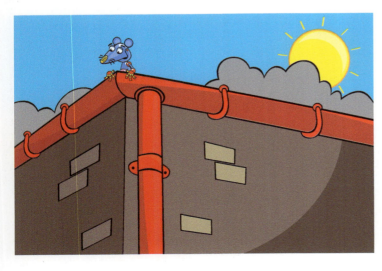
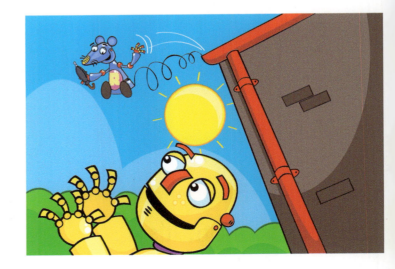

4. Animals

LESSON 1

1 Listen, point and repeat.

2 Listen and chant. 4.1

LESSON 2

3 Listen, say and color.

4 Listen and write ✓ or ✗.

can = ✓
can't = ✗

LESSON 3

5 Listen and circle. 4.2

6 Read and stick.

It can't climb trees.
It can't fly. It can swim.

It can run.
It can jump.

It can't run. It can't fly.
It can't swim.

31

At the Zoo!

LESSON 4

7 Listen to the story.

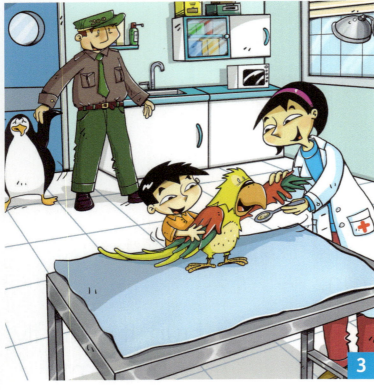

LESSON 5

8 Listen and complete.

9 Listen and sing.

Can a penguin fly in the sky, sky, sky?
No, it can't! No, it can't! No, it can't!

Can a penguin swim in the sea, sea, sea?
Yes, it can! Yes, it can! Yes, it can!

CLIL

LESSON 6

10 Read and stick.

This is a tiger-dile!
It's black and orange.
It can run.

This is an ele-bird.
It's green and red.
It can fly.

This is a zeb-phin.
It's black and white.
It can swim.

11 Read and draw.

This is a mon-cat.
It's brown and orange.
It can climb trees.

35

PHONICS

Beep's World!

LESSON 7

12 Listen. 4.6

5. Jobs

LESSON 1

1 Listen, point and repeat.

2 Listen and chant.

LESSON 2

3 Listen and number.

4 Play a game.

LESSON 3

5 Listen and sing. 5.3

A, B, C, 1, 2, 3,
Jobs for you and jobs for me.

6 Play a game.

The Firefighters!

LESSON 4

7 Listen to the story.

LESSON 5

8 Listen and chant. 5.5

Charlene's a chef.
Charlene's a chef.
She has a big white hat.

9 Read and match.

1 He has a violin.

2 He has a blue and white ball.

3 She has a big white hat.

4 He has lots of books.

5 She has a red nose.

42

CLIL

LESSON 6

10 Listen and stick. 5.6

firefighter

teacher

11 Draw and write.

I'm a _____.

43

Beep's World!

PHONICS

LESSON 7

12 Listen. 5.7

44

6. My Free Time

LESSON 1

1 Listen, point and repeat.

2 Listen and chant. 6.1

45

LESSON 2

3 Read and stick.

I'm listening to music.

I'm reading.

I'm painting.

I'm playing computer games.

4 Listen and circle.

1

2

46

LESSON 3

5 Listen and sing.

What are you doing today?
What are you doing today?
There's lots of fun for everyone.
So clap your hands and shout hooray!

6 Look and stick.

The Cake Competition!

LESSON 4

7 Listen to the story.

48

5

6

7

8

LESSON 5

8 Listen and circle. 🔘 6.5

9 Listen and sing. 6.6

Are you reading? Are you reading?
Yes, I am. Yes, I am.
Stories, books and comics.
Stories, books and comics.
Clap your hands, clap your hands.

CLIL

LESSON 6

10 Listen and number.

11 Draw your hobby.

Hi! My name's _____. My hobby is _____.

PHONICS

Beep's World!

LESSON 7

12 Listen. 6.8

7. The School Garden

LESSON 1

1 Listen, point and repeat.

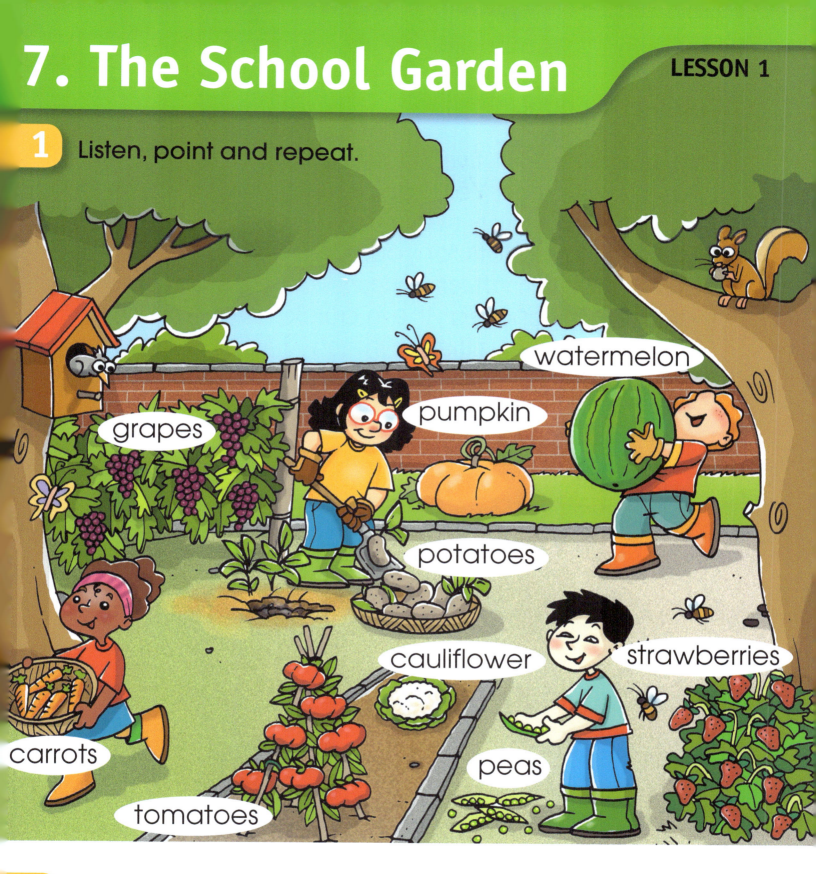

2 Count and match.

LESSON 2

3 Listen and chant.

One, two, three, four, five, six, seven.
I like strawberries! Yes, I do.
Eight, nine, ten, eleven, twelve.
Lots for me and lots for you.
Thirteen, fourteen, fifteen, sixteen.
Pick them all and eat them quick.
Seventeen, eighteen, nineteen, twenty.
Oh no! I feel sick!

4 Count and stick.

19 nineteen

15 fifteen

54

LESSON 3

5 Listen and circle. 7.2

6 Count and ask.

How many can you see?

The Enormous Pumpkin!

LESSON 4

7 Listen to the story.

56

LESSON 5

8 Listen and number.

9 Listen and sing.

In our school garden,
There are butterflies and bees.
Small green frogs in the pond,
And big, big, big tall trees.

CLIL

LESSON 6

10 Read and number.

1 It's pink. It can't run.

2 It's black and yellow. It can fly.

3 It's small and brown.

4 It's orange and purple. It can fly.

11 Listen and say. 7.6

1 Does a bee have eyes?

2 Does a worm have legs?

3 Does a snail have ears?

PHONICS

Beep's World!

LESSON 7

12 Listen. 🔊 7.7

8. The School Show

LESSON 1

1 Listen, point and repeat.

2 Listen and chant. 8.1

61

LESSON 2

3 Color, listen and point.

4 Listen and sing.

Can you ride a bike? Yes, I can.
Can you roller-blade?
Yes, I can, can, can.
Can you play basketball?
And sing a song?
Yes, I can. Yes, I can. Yes, I can.

LESSON 3

5 Listen and write ✓ or ✗.

			My friend
Can you juggle?	✗		
Can you ride a bike?			
Can you roller-blade?			
Can you play the recorder?			

6 Ask a friend.

The Magic Trick!

LESSON

7 Listen to the story.

1

2

3

4

64

LESSON 5

8 Look and stick.

9 Listen and sing.

I can play the guitar,
And I can ride a bike.
These are two things I really like.
I can roller-blade and I can climb up high,
But I just can't fly in the sky.

CLIL

LESSON 6

10 Look, read and number.

1 I can jump on a trampoline.
2 I can juggle five things.
3 I can ride a small bike.
4 I can stand on my hands.

11 Listen and color.

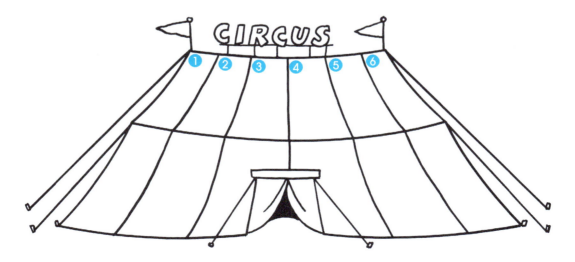

67

Beep's World!

PHONICS

LESSON 7

12 Listen. 8.7

Festivals

Halloween

1 Look and stick.

2 Listen and sing.

69

Christmas

1 Look and count.

 stars ☐ 🎁 presents ☐  angels ☐ 🔔 bells ☐

2 Listen and sing.

70

Carnival

1 Listen and color.

2 Listen and sing.

71

1 Match and say.

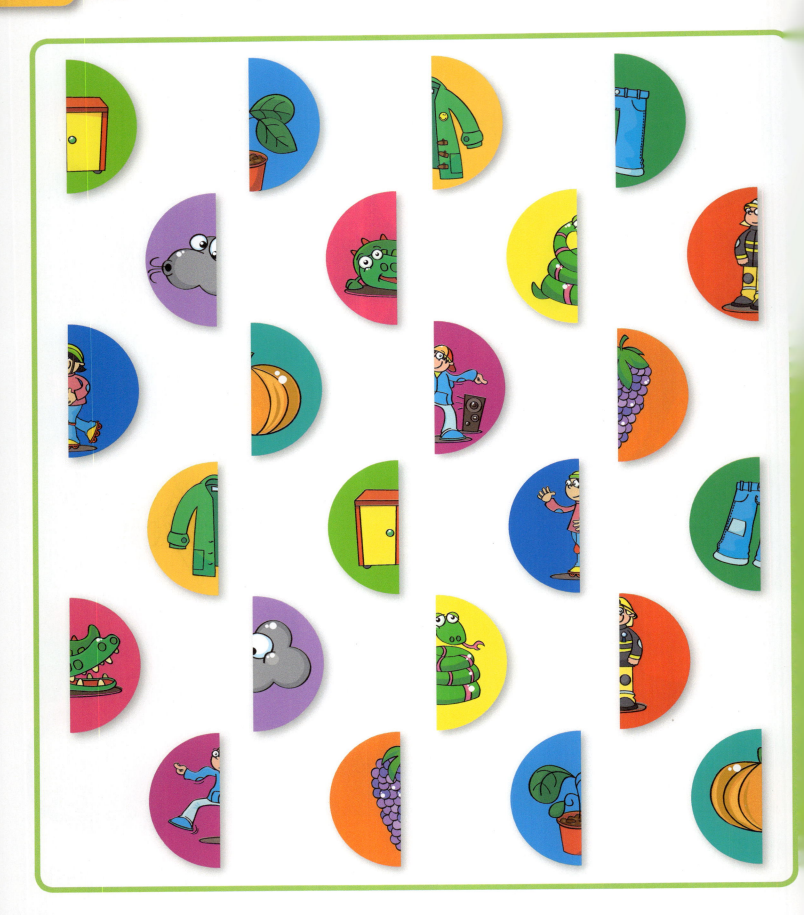

72

Activity Book

Contents

0 Welcome back!......2

1 Time for School......3

2 My Clothes......5

3 The Weather......7

4 Animals......9

5 Jobs......11

6 My Free Time......13

7 The School Garden......15

8 The School Show......17

Festivals......19

Picture Dictionary......22

Track List......31

Welcome back!

1 Match and write.

Ruby

Charlie

Monica

Lee

Chippy

2 Read and color.

Color four balls.

Color seven apples.

Color five parrots.

Color nine kites.

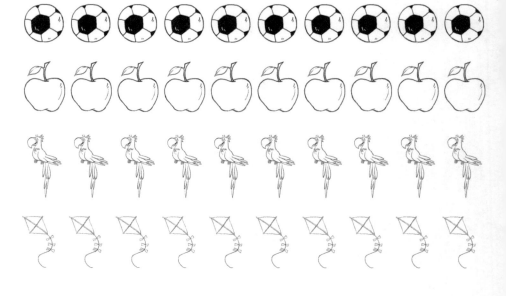

1. Time for School

1 Look and write.

on   under   in   behind

Where's the car?

_____   _____   _____   _____

2 Read and draw.

The pencil is in the schoolbag.

The ruler is in the cupboard.

The teddy bear is under the chair.

The sharpener is on the chair.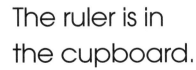

The ball is behind the plant.

The car is on the bookcase.

Review

1 Match and write.

1. cupboard t _ _ sh c _ n

2. trash can _ o _ p _ t e _

3. window c _ p _ o _ _ d

4. computer _ o o _ c _ _ e

5. bookcase _ i _ d _ w

2 Look and write.

on   under   in   behind

 The snake is _____ the chair.

 The cake is _____ the table.

 The elephant is _____ the plant.

 The cat is _____ the schoolbag.

2. My Clothes

1 Read and circle.

1 Are you wearing pants?   **Yes / No**

2 Are you wearing a dress?   **Yes / No**

3 Are you wearing a T-shirt?   **Yes / No**

4 Are you wearing shoes?   **Yes / No**

5 Are you wearing a sweater?   **Yes / No**

6 Are you wearing shorts?   **Yes / No**

2 Draw yourself and write.

I'm wearing _____

Review

1 Look and write.

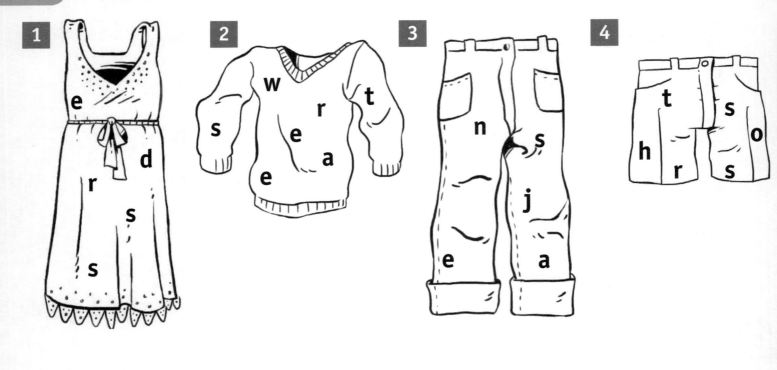

_____ _____ _____ _____

2 Read and complete.

(hat   jeans   shorts)

I'm wearing _____ and a sweater.

I'm wearing a dress and a _____.

I'm wearing _____ and a T-shirt.

3. The Weather

1 Find, circle and write.

k	r	a	i	n	i	n	g
w	i	n	d	y	e	a	k
a	s	c	o	l	d	o	p
s	n	o	w	i	n	g	e
d	o	g	s	u	n	n	y
e	m	c	l	o	u	d	y

It's _____.

It's _____.

It's _____.

It's _____.

It's _____.

It's _____.

2 Draw and write.

What's the weather like today?

_____

Review

1 Look and write.

> snowing   hot   windy   sunny   cold   raining

It's _____ and it's _____.   It's _____ and it's _____.   It's _____ and it's _____.

2 Read and color.

Put on your yellow T-shirt and blue shorts.

Put on your red hat and green coat.

8

4. Animals

1 Read and circle.

It can fly.   It can't jump.   It can't climb.

2 Look and write.

can ✓   can't ✗

It __can't__ run.   It _____ climb.   It _____ jump.

It _____ fly.   It _____ run.   It _____ fly.

Review

1 Look and complete.

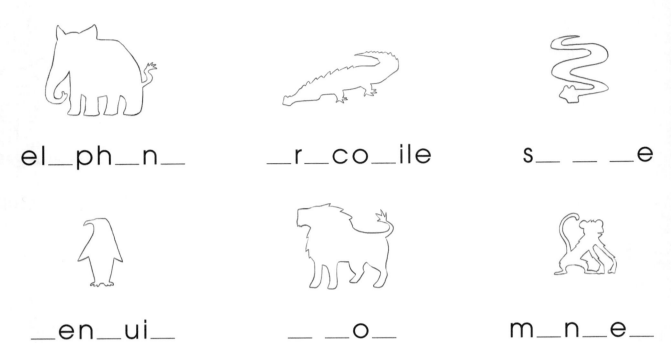

el_ph_n_   _r_co_ile   s_ _ _e

_en_ui_   _ _o_   m_n_e_

2 Look and write.

fly   climb   run   swim

A zebra can _____.   A zebra can't _____.

A penguin can _____.   A penguin can't _____.

5. Jobs

1 Read and color.

He has a red and blue T-shirt.

She has a blue and yellow bus.

She has a purple guitar.

She has a yellow hat.

2 Look and complete.

> He has   She has

1

_____ a computer.

2

_____ a bike.

3

_____ a big book.

4

_____ a cat.

Review

1 Look and write.

_____   _____   _____   _____

2 Look and write.

He's a	chef.	firefighter.
	doctor.	bus driver.
She's a	musician.	nurse.

1    2    3

4    5    6

6. My Free Time

1 Look and write.

1.

My hobby is playing _____.

2.

My hobby is _____.

3.

My hobby is _____.

4.

My hobby is _____.

2 Read and complete.

listening   favorite   name

Hello!
My _____ 's Mark.
My hobby is _____
to music. My _____
music is rap.
What's your hobby?

13

Review

1 Complete the words.

_istening   _ra_in_   _e_di_g   _a_c_ng
_o _usic

2 Write.

computer   I'm   games
playing

_____.

book   reading   I'm
a

_____.

TV   watching   I'm

_____.

soccer   I'm   playing

_____.

7. The School Garden

1 Look and color.

big = yellow   small = green

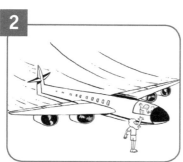

2 Look and write.

They're big.   They're small.

_____   _____

_____   _____

15

Review

1 Find and write.

a	s	q	w	c	z	v	x	p	k	c
k	t	o	m	a	t	o	e	s	x	a
b	r	n	q	r	w	p	e	p	r	u
w	a	t	e	r	m	e	l	o	n	l
z	w	x	c	o	v	a	b	t	q	i
m	b	n	b	t	v	s	c	a	x	f
p	e	o	i	s	u	y	t	t	r	l
w	r	q	x	o	r	a	t	o	e	o
a	r	s	d	f	g	h	j	e	k	w
q	i	w	g	r	a	p	e	s	e	e
t	e	q	w	z	x	s	a	q	z	r
k	s	z	p	u	m	p	k	i	n	o

8. The School Show

1 Look and write.

> juggle   play basketball   roller-blade   ride a bike

2 Read and write.

> Yes, I can.   No, I can't.

1.  Can you do gymnastics? _____

2. Can you play the recorder? _____

3. Can you sing? _____

17

Review

1 Circle and write.

juggle play the recorder sing do gymnastics ride a bike roller-blade

2 Complete.

I can   I can't   juggle   sing   play basketball   roller-blade

Festivals

Halloween

1 Match and write.

skeleton

witch

pumpkin

spider

ghost

2 Read and color.

1 = black
2 = purple
3 = green
4 = red
5 = orange
6 = yellow

19

Christmas

1 Draw, color and write.

> present   snowman   star   bell   angel   tree

_ _ _ _ _ _   _ _ _ _ _ _   _ _ _ _ _ _

_ _ _ _ _ _   _ _ _ _ _ _   _ _ _ _ _ _

2 Look and circle.

doll / teddy bear   car / train   bike / plane   kite / ball

20

Carnival

1 Read and color.

- dress → pink
- shoes → red
- coat → purple
- sweater → green
- pants → black
- hat → yellow

2 Draw and write.

I'm wearing _____.

21

Picture Dictionary 1

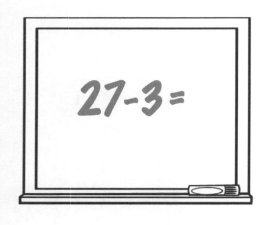  

board   bookcase   computer

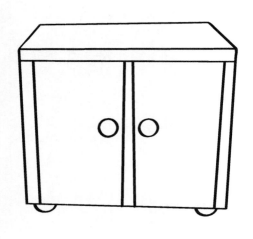 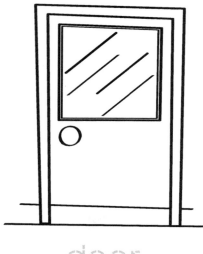 

cupboard   door   plant

teacher   trash can   window

Picture Dictionary 2

coat dress hat jacket

jeans pants shoes

shorts sweater T-shirt

Picture Dictionary 3

It's cloudy.   It's cold.   It's hot.

It's raining.   It's snowing.

It's sunny.   It's windy.

Picture Dictionary 4

bird   crocodile   elephant

lion   monkey   penguin

snake   tiger   zebra

Picture Dictionary 5

bus driver

chef

doctor

firefighter

musician

nurse

pilot

soccer player

Picture Dictionary 6

dancing   drawing   listening to music

painting   playing computer games   playing soccer

reading   watching TV

27

Picture Dictionary 7

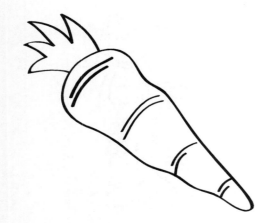

carrot   cauliflower   grapes

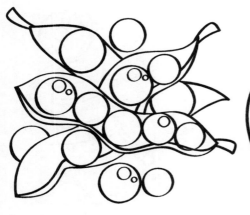
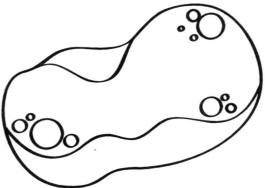

peas   potato   pumpkin

strawberry   tomato   watermelon

Picture Dictionary 8

do gymnastics   do karate   juggle

play basketball   play the recorder   ride a bike

roller-blade   sing

29

1 Look at the leaves, add a word and write the unit number.

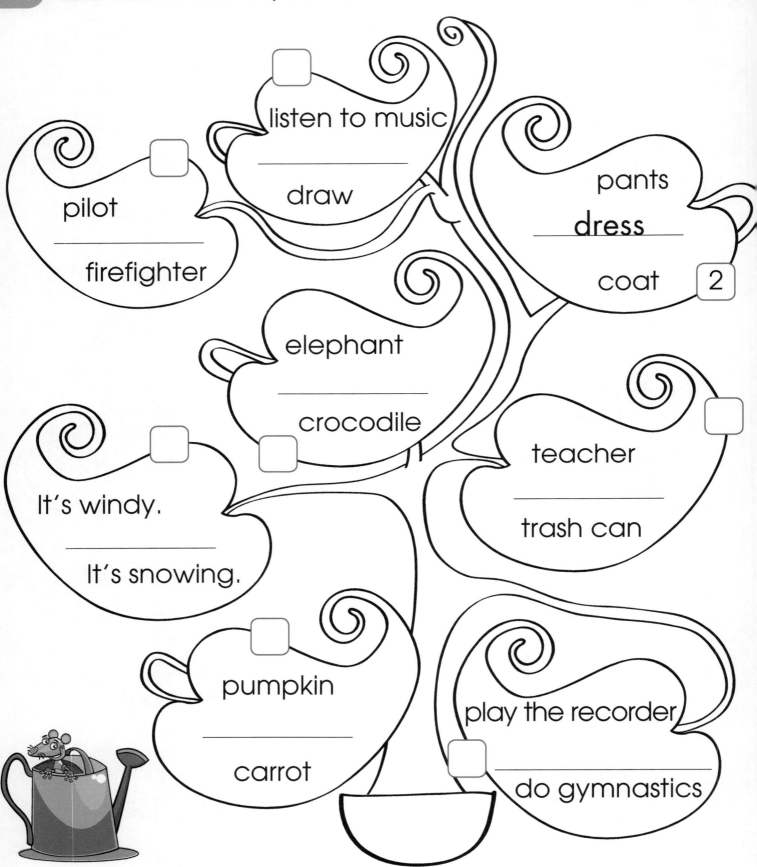

30

Track List

Student's Book
Songs, chants and stories

Track	Transcript	
Unit 0		
1	0.2	Chant: How are you?
2	0.4	Song: Favorite Things
Unit 1		
3	1.1	Chant: One, Two, Three, Four, Point!
4	1.3	Chant: Where's the hamster?
5	1.4	Story: Hide and Seek!
6	1.5	Song: The Alphabet Song
7	1.7	Beep's World!
Unit 2		
8	2.3	Chant: What are you wearing today?
9	2.4	Story: Monica's Party!
10	2.5	Song: Are you wearing green shoes?
11	2.6	Beep's World!
Unit 3		
12	3.1	Chant: The Weather Chant
13	3.3	Song: What's the weather like?
14	3.4	Story: The Snowman!
15	3.6	Chant: Is it cold today?
16	3.7	Beep's World!
Unit 4		
17	4.1	Chant: Animals in My House!
18	4.3	Story: At the Zoo!
19	4.5	Song: Can a penguin fly?
20	4.6	Beep's World!
Unit 5		
21	5.1	Chant: The People That You Meet
22	5.3	Song: Jobs for You and Jobs for Me
23	5.4	Story: The Firefighters!
24	5.5	Chant: Charlene's a chef.
25	5.7	Beep's World!
Unit 6		
26	6.1	Chant: So Many Things to Do
27	6.3	Song: What are you doing today?
28	6.4	Story: The Cake Competition!
29	6.6	Song: Are you reading?
30	6.8	Beep's World!

Track	Transcript	
Unit 7		
31	7.1	Chant: The Numbers Chant
32	7.3	Story: The Enormous Pumpkin!
33	7.5	Song: Our School Garden
34	7.7	Beep's World!
Unit 8		
35	8.1	Chant: Ride a bike.
36	8.3	Song: What can you do?
37	8.5	Story: The Magic Trick!
38	8.6	Song: I just can't fly!
39	8.7	Beep's World!
Festivals		
40	F1	Song: The Halloween Song
41	F2	Song: The Christmas Song
42	F4	Song: It's Carnival!

Activity Book
Picture Dictionary

Track	Transcript	
43	PD1	Picture Dictionary 1
44	PD2	Picture Dictionary 2
45	PD3	Picture Dictionary 3
46	PD4	Picture Dictionary 4
47	PD5	Picture Dictionary 5
48	PD6	Picture Dictionary 6
49	PD7	Picture Dictionary 7
50	PD8	Picture Dictionary 8